Raising Lazarus

A journey to discover a British West Indian who served in World War 1

Kat François

GWAA, TSL Publications

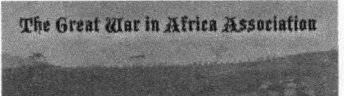

First published in Great Britain in 2016
By ZupaKat Publications

This edition, 2023, published
By GWAA, TSL Publications, Rickmansworth

Copyright © 2023 Kat François

ISBN / 978-1-915660-33-6

The right of Kat François to be identified as the playwright/author of this work has been asserted by the authors in accordance with the UK Copyright, Designs and Patents Act 1988.

All rights reserved. No part of this publication may be reproduced, stored in a retrieval system or transmitted, in any form or by any means without the prior written permission of the publisher, nor be otherwise circulated in any form of binding or cover other than that in which it is published and without a similar condition being imposed on the subsequent buyer.

Some names and places have been changed to respect the family's privacy.

Rights of performance

Rights of performance for these scripts are controlled by TSL Publications (tslbooks.uk/Drama) which issues a performing licence on payment of a fee and subject to a number of conditions (specified on tslbooks.uk/Drama). These scripts are fully protected under the Copyright Laws of the British Commonwealth of Nations, the United States of America and all countries of the Berne and Universal Copyright Conventions. All rights, including Online, Stage, Motion Picture, Radio, Television, Public Reading and Translation into Foreign Languages are strictly reserved. It is an infringement of the Copyright to give any performance or public reading of these scripts before the fee has been paid and the licence issued. The Royalty Fee is subject to contract and subject to variation at the sole discretion of TSL Publications. In Territories Overseas the fees quoted may not apply. A fee will be quoted on application to TSL Publications.

Cover image: Robert Covell

Visit katfrancois.com for further information

DEDICATED TO

Dedicated to Miss Joyce Harrison, granddaughter of Lazarus François and his great granddaughter Ava.

Cousin Bertine who I met in Grenada in 2009 and who has since passed away.

My gran, Mary François, for being so open and willing to pass on the family history to me.

To Dawn Reid who originally directed *Raising Lazarus* and who has always supported my writing and performance career.

To my mum, Ann François, for her love of history and her encouragement in all I do.

To my siblings Rachel, Curtis, Emma, Danny, Mari, Richie as well as the rest of my family, aunties, uncles, cousins, and friends who continue to tirelessly support the work I do.

To Robert Covell who started this whole journey and has been with me every step of the way.

To everyone who has ever seen *Raising Lazarus*, supported *Raising Lazarus*, put *Raising Lazarus* on, without you this story could not be told.

To the organisations who have supported and continue to support this important story.

Lastly to Lazarus François and to all the Caribbean soldiers who volunteered to fight when Britain needed them. To all the soldiers across the Empire who have responded every time the Motherland has called, may your stories never be forgotten.

Creative team

Writer/performer: Kat François
Director: Dawn Reid
Stage Manager, Researcher and technical support: Robert Covell

Raising Lazarus was first developed in a project
called Spoke Lab at
The Theatre Royal Stratford East
in 2010.

It has since been performed at
Camden Roundhouse London, Nottingham Play House, Rich Mix London, Decibel Manchester, KPMG Docklands, Imperial War Museum London, The Hawth Crawley, The Camden Fringe Festival London, Attenborough Centre for the Creative Arts for the Brighton Festival. *Raising Lazarus* has also been performed in Germany, Canada, Australia and South Africa, and will continue to tour internationally.

Writer/actress

Kat François

Kat François is a Performance Artist and Writer, Creative Wellbeing Coach, Education Consultant in the Arts and PHSE (personal, social, health and economic), as well as Writing and Performance Coach.

She was the first person to win a televised poetry slam in the UK, and later went on to win the World Slam Poetry Championships, held in Rotterdam. She has performed her acclaimed poetry and theatre pieces across the world.

A well-known performance poet on the London poetry scene, Kat hosted a monthly poetry and music event, Word4Word, for 15 years at Theatre Royal Stratford East.

As a playwright, Kat has written and performed two solo plays, *Seven Times Me*, *Raising Lazarus*, and three solo comedy shows.

Kat has worked with young people for many years, in many different roles, such as a youth worker, running PHSE workshops, as well as teaching dance, drama, poetry, and performance skills. She is an experienced director of youth theatre, devising plays for theatres including Theatre Royal Stratford East, Roundhouse Camden, Lyric Theatre Hammersmith, as well as directing performances at Arcola Theatre, and Camp Bestival.

Kat mentors young performers and writers, regularly leading workshops to help develop their skills as well as devising and directing work they've created.

Kat holds weekly online 'Writing for Wellbeing' workshops for marginalised women.

Kat has appeared numerous times on radio and television, including Blue Peter, the Big Poetry Slam, BBC Breakfast TV, SKY 1 and Sky Arts, BBC Radio 4's Front Row, Woman's Hour and Saturday Live, including BBC commissions. Kat has also been commissioned to write and perform by both corporate and community organisations.

Kat is published in several poetry magazines and anthologies. Her first written collection of poetry, *Rhyme and Reason*, was published in February 2008 and is now in its third edition.

Raising Lazarus the play, has been performed in South Africa, Germany, Canada and Australia as well as all over the UK, receiving a four-star review at Brighton Festival. The play was also invited to be performed as part of the Night Before The Somme centenary commemorative event at the Imperial War Museum, London 2016.

The play is still available for performances. Kat has created an in-school version of the play that can be performed in the classroom and is suitable for ages 9 upwards, with accompanying workshops.

For more information visit katfrancois.com

Raising Lazarus

Characters

1. Kat François
2. Lazarus François
3. Gran
4. Dosue
5. Nurse Burton
6. Delvin Sharpe, Army Recruiter

Performance Notes

Raising Lazarus is a one-act play set in two separate time zones, 1915-1916 and the year 2009.

The play is set in 3 different countries: England, Grenada and Egypt.

The play consists of 22 mini scenes.

The end of the play is usually followed by Q & A, with Kat François.

Running time

Approx 60 minutes
plus Q & A typically an additional 30 minutes

Scene 1

Lights up.

Mother's, Mother's land 2009

KAT: Grenada my mother's, mother's land
was wrapped up in childhood stories
of mango trees as tall as mountains
ripe with burnt fruit
rugby shaped and delicious
of sticky pulp shoved into eager mouths
of snakes as long as rope
as thick as muscular arms
camouflaged
waiting to scare greedy children
from their branches
of days spent, gallivanting with fellow village children
playing hide and seek in sugar cane fields
which swallowed small and nimble bodies.

Grenada my mother's, mother's land
lived in the spice box
in the middle of dark nutmeg marbles
and strips of bark
which smelt not of tree but of cinnamon
in the hotness of fiery seasoning
which was the catalyst
for mini fire works on the tips of tongues
in the cool long glasses of sarsaparilla
we thirstily gulped.

Grenada my mother's, mother's land
stared out from curiously coloured pictures
which sat regally on the mantelpiece
it was a faraway, exotic place
full of brown skinned inhabitants

surrounded by the bluest water
which sparkled under the heat of the Caribbean sun
it snuck into our English house
and slipped ghost-like into our dreams
reminding us of where we really belonged
Grenada my mother's, mother's land
grew up in the house beside us
an invisible eighth sibling.

SCENE 2

Do you have a relative who fought in the First Word War?

KAT: Hi thank you all for coming, my name's Kat François. I knew nothing about Lazarus until October 2008 when I booked a trip to Grenada. It was to be my third visit, and that was around the time I'd also just received confirmation of my place in the London marathon. I'd always wanted to run the marathon, my clothes were starting to get a bit tight again, and although extreme, was my way of getting fit and healthy.

Mum would be coming to Grenada as would my boyfriend. It would be his first visit and he decided to brush up on his knowledge. He picked up a book called *Grenada a History of Its People*, by Beverley Steele. Whilst reading it, he called me over and pointed at a picture, a picture of a memorial, then he pointed at a name C.L. François.

He asked me "Do you have a relative who fought in the First World War?"

I became instantly vexed. "No of course not. If I did I would know about it, wouldn't I, wouldn't I? He must be related to some other François family."

I was angry because I did not want to even think about the fact that I could be so ignorant about such an important piece of family history.

So I pushed the picture to the back of my mind, out right rejected any thought of C.L. François, as far as I was concerned, there was no way he could be a relative of mine.

It was not until months later whilst packing a barrel of clothes, toys, shoes and books to send ahead of me before my visit to Grenada did Lazarus cross my mind again.

I called Mum, but she'd never heard of a relative fighting in the First World War, so she told me to speak to gran who at 77 is a wealth of family information.

SCENE 3

A visit to Gran.

GRAN: Come in, come in, so good to see you, Let me see that book, where the picture there? C.L. François, I am not sure what the C stands for but I know him as Lazarus François and yes, yes he's related to us, but Bonjay it's a long, long, long, long time since I hear that name.

I didn't know, a memorial, in St George's, you never hear me mention Lazarus before, you sure, want some tea? No, okay just ask if you want anything.

Lazarus and your great grandpopha, my faddah was first cousin, let me say that again. Lazarus and your great grandfaddah, my popha was first cousin. The two of dem, both went to sign up for the army together but they only take Lazarus, they say my popha had too many dependents. I guess dem right, well in the end he did have 11 children altogether, your great grandfaddah was a good looking man, tall, dark, a good head of hair, I can't really blame my muddah.

Lazarus, no sorry, I don't know what Lazarus look like but dey say he was teacher, a good teacher and that he had a strong mind, he wasn't a *cunumoonu*, you know what a cunumoonu is? Well it's a foolish man, a man who let woman run rings around him.

Lazarus was not that kind of man, he had one woman who he loved, what she name ... it's there, it's there, it's there, that's it, that's it, that's it, Dosue, Dosue was her name, but she real name was Bernadette. I don't know why we Grenadians bother christening anybody, when we never call him or her by his or her real name.

Dosue and Lazarus had one child, Theresa, but she passed a while back, Theresa had two children, a boy, a doctor, but he dead in a car accident and a data she alive though, Joyce I think she name is, she living in the States, you want me to see if I can get in contact with her for you? It would be good for you to talk to her cause she has to know more than me.

I have some chicken soup boiling there you know, you don't want any? Oh I forget you are a vegetarian, I sorry to hear that, I hope you get better soon.

I can't believe you didn't know about Lazarus, at least your mother should've known about him being born back home. They say he might have spent time in France and England.

Eh, I get it now, him want you to raise him, Lazarus want you to raise him, don't laugh, don't laugh, I don't making joke with you, you have to find out what happen to him, tell he story, why else, why else would you come across the picture, you is the poet in the family, the writer, the story-teller, the performer, of course it's you he choose, I get it now, it all make perfect sense.

You want some fruitcake? I know you like your fruitcake … no okay, mind you don't disappear, you English children always on diet.

SCENE 4

I wish I'd known.

KAT: So I was related to Lazarus, I was related to Lazarus François, First World War soldier, any questions or doubt had been completely blown away.

A funny feeling jumped into my stomach, a tiny piece of excitement blended with a dash of fear, this was huge. I didn't take on board the spirituality stuff Gran was talking about, but even I had to admit this whole thing was out of the ordinary, especially his name Lazarus. Now I don't remember all my Sunday school stories, but wasn't he the guy who Jesus raised from the dead? What was bothering me most, how comes Gran had never mentioned him before, how comes I'd never heard the family talk of him?

How comes I was never taught anything about the British West Indies Regiment? As a kid I hated history, could just about keep my eyes open during history lessons, we learnt about William the Conqueror, the War of the Roses, Tudors, Oliver Cromwell, Henry the Eighth and all the damn wives he divorced, or killed off, the Edwardians, the Victorians, the suffragettes, even slavery and every black history month, they dusted off and rolled out Martin Luther King and Rosa Parks, but never, ever did we learn about the contribution the Caribbean made to the First or even the Second World War. Where were our photos, our films, our documentaries, and our memorials? I wished I'd known.

I wish I'd known about Lazarus
when the National Front
invaded my high street
marching, shouting, chanting
eyes cold, attitude bold
racist leaflets in hand
shorn hair and red laces, their NF brand.

I wish I'd known about Lazarus
when I was called a black pig
by a pink faced, blonde-haired, blue-eyed
girl in my primary school class
who thought it would be fun
to call me names
thought it would be fun
t laugh at my race
who thought it was fun
until I slapped her and put her in her place.

I wish I'd known about Lazarus
when the primary school head teacher
would always cane the black boys
never the white boys
or when he sent the police to my house
for stealing a few rubbers, a few pens
would always come down heavily
on those of us from a West Indian background
never any leeway or kindness found.

I wish I'd known about Lazarus
when old English people would say
"Go back to where you come from."
or "My grandfather didn't fight for this country
for it to be overrun by your sort."

I wish I'd known about Lazarus
when those six police officers
forced me to the ground
manhandling, laughing, physically manipulating
handcuffing, into the back of a van throwing

almost succeeding in suffocating
even though it was a case of mistaken identity
no remorse
until taken to the courts
stopped those racist thoughts
I wish I'd known, I wish I'd known
I wish I'd known.

SCENE 5

A call from Joyce

[*Audio of a telephone ringing.*]

KAT: Joyce called, Lazarus' granddaughter, bwoy Gran works super fast, not even got my head around the facts and yet there I was talking to his granddaughter, who was emotional, I mean really emotional, crying, laughing, thanking me for searching for her grandfather. The joy in her voice made me wish I'd started the search earlier. Joyce is of retirement age and lives in America.

She said Lazarus was a teacher, she said Lazarus was an outspoken man, she said she thinks he spent time in France and England, she said that her mother, Theresa, Lazarus' daughter was only three years old when he left.

She said Lazarus gave a will to Dosue, which she kept stuffed in her pillow.

Talking, talking, talking, half-crying, half-laughing, still touched, thanking, thanking, thanking me, even though I have yet to out find anything of use. It's going to take a while to figure out what's fact and what's fiction.

I promise to keep in touch, talking to her has made Lazarus more than just an anonymous name on a cold memorial, he's a real person, he's family. That's it, I'm on it, one hundred and fifty percent.

First stop, National Archives, whom I contact online. I request the war diaries of the British West Indies Regiment. It should tell me all I need to know about where they went, what they done – here look [*Kat picks up a laminate of the war diary, which is also shown on a slide, to the audience*] the war diaries are a day-to-day break down of the soldiers' activities, marching, drill, musketry training.

I also request Lazarus' medal records from the National Archives, but he doesn't have any medals, not even one, never mind. [*A visual of the war diary is shown to the audience.*]

I devour anything I can find, on the net, I read the book that started it all, with the picture of the memorial and this book, which became my bible, *A Social History of the West Indies in the First World War*. [*Kat picks up the book and shows it to the audience.*]

There were other books but they were not easy to come by, they are either out of print, or way too expensive. I wanted to know, what the conditions were like, how England treated them, if Lazarus got to see any action, but the first thing I wanted to know was why, why would anyone want to go and fight for a country that wasn't theirs to fight for?

SCENE 6

Recruitment 1915

BROTHER DELVIN SHARPE   This is Brother Delvin Sharpe, community leader, church treasurer and army recruiter, sending a message to all young Grenadian men.

There comes a time in a man's life when he has to make a decision to either sit back, be idle and do nothing or take a once in a lifetime opportunity to prove how brave he is.

If I myself was young enough I would not hesitate to offer my services. The Motherland needs you; England needs Grenadians, to help her in her endeavours against the evil that is Germany. Let us send forth as many courageous, fearless and indomitable men as we can, and prove to the Motherland that we her loyal and faithful subjects are willing and able to offer our undying support in her time of dire need.

We are aiming to put together a contingent of men to send overseas as soon as possible. We are looking for young men who will proudly represent Grenada and the West Indies.

We are looking for young men who are seeking to improve and better themselves. We are looking for young men who are not afraid of hard toil.

That's it, step forward, step forward, sign up, sign up to the British West Indies Regiment. You will be greatly rewarded for your efforts. You will be paid the same as the English soldiers and you will receive a pension.

You will have the chance to educate and develop yourself, travel and learn new skills. That's it, step forward, step forward, sign up, sign up to the British West Indies Regiment. You will return as heroes, you will make your families and your country eternally proud.

I implore you to join the British West Indies Regiment. Do not let it be said that Grenadians did not do their part for King and for country.

SCENE 7

Dosue 1915

DOSUE: Papa Jay Laza we're don't even marry yet and you leaving me? Don't Dosue darling me, you chupid or something, you lost all your sense, ah should've listen to my popha he said you was no good. Don't touch me, it was your touching that get us in trouble in the first place, look how you walking away from me, you walking from your child.

Why go now, now that ah said I'd marry you, ah don't care what my popha thinks anymore, ah don't want anything to happen to you, why can't you see that?

Listen for one moment, just listen, my aunty said we can take the spare room she have there in the back, she doesn't mind, until we save up enough and can build our own house, it won't be for long.

Ah don't understand why you feel the need to go off and fight, how much of a big man you have to prove you are, you think that the beke man, the English, would come all the way over here to little old Grenada to fight for us? No, ah won't sssssh, why should ah be quiet when ah talking truth.

You can kill someone Lazarus? Cause that's what soldiers do and from what ah can remember you can just about kill a chicken. Ah sick of talking, bawling and begging, if you want to go, go, but don't think ah go be sitting around like a good little girl waiting for your no good backside to return, ah not waiting, ah not waiting at all, at all!

SCENE 8

Lazarus / SS Verdala *1915*

[*Slide of the troop ship SS* Verdala *displayed.*]

KAT: 21st August 1915, the first contingent of soldiers from Grenada depart on board the SS *Verdala*. This ship called at St Vincent where another 50 men joined the contingent making a total of 200.

They said goodbye to Caribbean soil
they said goodbye, family, friend and foe
they said goodbye burnt mangoes
ripe and moist from the sun so warm.

They said goodbye mother
they said goodbye father
they said goodbye to their children still small
they said goodbye to their children so small.

They said goodbye clear blue skies
they said goodbye to the Tamarind tree
full of fruit, sharp and sweet
they said goodbye to the bright sunshine
they said goodbye to lush green earth
they said goodbye to their place of birth.

They said goodbye
they said goodbye
they said goodbye.

[*Addressing the audience.*]

LAZARUS: Private Lazarus Emmanuel Louis François, serial number 842, people was line up, line up everywhere, bouncing each other out of the way, just to get a good spot, brass band, dignitaries, family, friends, so much people, mudha and faddah waving, muddah crying, no Dosue.

[*Addressing a fellow soldier.*]

Hold on, hold on, oh gosh, don't cheat me, I coming, I coming, the domino king is coming,

[*Addressing the audience.*]

Some men on these boat, can't take the rocking, spend most of the three weeks with their head over the side of the boats, spilling up their gut, make everything smell foul, foul.

[*Addressing a fellow soldier.*]

Stop you chupidness, I know it's a double four you have there, it's only you that could have it, play it man, play it.

[*Addressing the audience.*}

You see the boy over there, yes the one staring, staring out into the ocean, he searching for submarine, terrified, he terrified of getting torpedoed. Being on a boat for three weeks can do funny things to a man.

Hey you boy, yes you, come, come, move from there, no sense worrying, if we get torpedoed there is nothing you can do, Bonjay, you see what I mean, no one can convince him to move.

[*Addressing a fellow soldier.*]

Oh gosh, oh gosh, oh gosh, you cheating me, just cause I talking don't mean I can't see what you are doing, I still paying attention you know.

[*Addressing the audience.*]

I can't wait to reach England, since I a little boy in short pants, dream I dream of going to the Motherland, everyone here on this boat can't wait to reach the Motherland, all kind of men on this boat you know, farmer, baker, electrician, carpenter, policeman, and teachers just like me, all after the same ting, a chance to fight on behalf of the Motherland and a chance to mash up dem Germans, good and proper.

[*Addressing a fellow solider.*]

You throwing double six, ehh, ehh, I see what kind of game you playing, you think you smart? Well you don't smarter than me.

[*Addressing the audience.*]

They won't know what hit them when us West Indian boys get a chance to fight. We go work hard, hard, we go be the best soldiers we can be, we don't fraid hard work, you know, no, no we don't fraid hard work at all, at all.

Three more weeks to go, the first thing I go do when I get off this boat, is get down on my hands and knees, kiss the ground and thank the Lord I reach safe.

[*Addressing a fellow soldier.*]

There you go, double blank, you could never beat the domino king, how many times I have to buss all you up for you to learn that.

[*Addressing the audience.*]

I wonder what the English will think of us when we reach, this boat full of black soldiers.

We are jolly West Indian soldiers
as jolly as jolly can be
and we going to fight for England
across the raging sea
we are jolly West Indian soldiers
as jolly as jolly can be
and we going to beat the Kaiser up
and bring him to his knees
We are jolly West Indian soldiers
as jolly as jolly can be
and we going to mash up Germany
before she mash up we
and we going to mash up Germany
before she mash up weeeeeeeeeeee!

[*Audio recitation of the following proclamation.*]

"War Office, 1915.
His Majesty the KING has been graciously pleased to approve of the formation of a Corps from contingents of the inhabitants of the West Indian islands, to be entitled *The British West Indies Regiment*.

The London Gazette 26th October 1915."

SCENE 9

Imperial War Museum 2009

[*Kat picks up two books one red, one black.*]

KAT: Imperial War Museum, Lambeth, London, archives room, never been there before, never had a need to. Typed British West Indies Regiment into the search computer, that's when Nurse Burton and her diaries popped up.

Minutes later, I'm sitting in front of two small autograph books, one black, one red, full of writing and drawings by West Indian soldiers and others who passed through her care, at Surrey House Convalescence Home, Seaford during the First World War.

[*Slide of the Surrey House Convalescence Home, displayed.*]

Carefully touch the yellowing sheets, imagining brown hands skimming across the pages when they were fresh white and clean. It's a compelling moment, library silence adding to the heavy feeling of responsibility that is beginning to weigh me down. All these names are names of soldiers with untold stories. There I was a poet, reading poetry written almost a hundred years ago, by Caribbean soldiers.

Sounds silly now, but yes I did search for Lazarus' name. There was a Lionel French, a George Arthur Bailey, a John Henry Sykes, Wonal Junior, Emmanuel Arneaud, and a Jacob Cunningham, but no Lazarus.

NURSE BURTON: Never seen a black person before, heard about them, read about them, even seen pictures but never seen one in the flesh and look at me now, here I am with hundreds of them. I'm Nurse Burton, feel sorry for them, poor buggers, being so far from home, poor things, must be difficult with the barracks being in such bad condition and the weather being so horrible, a lot of them are falling sick.

Don't think they cope with the cold very well, coming from somewhere so hot, they should've brought them over in the summer really, but what do I know, after all I'm only a nurse.

I try to make them as comfortable as I can, some of the white soldiers refuse to lie in a bed next to them and demand to be moved, bloody cheek, I move them all right, to somewhere real drafty.

A few of the nurses and orderlies are not very understanding as they could be, but I'm a God fearing woman who's been raised to see all humans as equal, I refuse to treat them any differently to our boys, after all, they have come all the way over here to fight for us.

Such polite young men and grateful, not one of them has given me a moment's trouble, and they speak such good English; many of them speak better than me.

Don't tell anyone I've said this, maybe I shouldn't say it, oh what the heck, some of those West Indian boys are very good looking and got such great ... You know ... physiques. Of course, I'm behaving myself, after all I am a nurse and they won't be here for very long so no sense getting a broken heart. I heard they're planning to ship them out to Egypt pretty soon, so they can finish their training somewhere warm and guard the Swizz, Swizz ... Suez canal.

Anyway I got my diaries to remember them by, mmmm let's see if I can find my favourite poem, yes, yes, here it is.

To Sister Burton,

I'm only a West Indian soldier
And I was dying as fast as can be
For my chest was racking with pain
That I thought wasn't natural to man
And though I can't find words to express it
I'm trying these few words to tell
About you kind sister of the Red Cross
May God bless, help you prosper well.

That's me he's talking about.

Dear sister you're one in a thousand
and I'll bless you with all this poor heart.
you know we're built like all humans
your kindness has done its part
so when out yonder I'm fighting
remember me please in your prayers
it isn't as strange, as you'd fancy
for my family remember me in theirs.

[*A poem from Nurse Burton's diary written by a soldier of the British West Indies Regiment.*]

Beautiful, isn't it? No one has ever written poetry just for me.

We lost another one yesterday, a real young one, pneumonia, only 22 years old, same age as my youngest brother. He held on for a few days, we really thought he was going to make it. We buried him in Seaford Cemetery. Nelson Fervier, from St Lucia. Can't stand to think how his mother will feel when she gets that horrible telegram, he told me that he was all she had.

I wish there was more we could've done for him; it shouldn't have happened. I can't bear the thought of him sleeping in a foreign land, covered by foreign dirt, no one to shed a tear or tell him he was brave, no one to tend to his grave. Better go, matron will be wondering where I've got to.

[*Video footage of Kat reciting a poem at Seaford Cemetery is played, the poem performed is transcribed below.*]

19 Men

Here they lay 19 West Indian Soldiers
the adventurous, the bold of World War One
a pile of old but not forgotten Caribbean bones
across the seas they came
to the Motherland's aid
to fight for King and to fight for country
dreaming of returning heroes
bursting full of boastful stories to share
medals on lapels
and pensions in their back pockets
families proud and happy to have them back home
bodies, limbs intact
but they did not return
they did not survive
the harsh English temperature defeated them
mumps and pneumonia ravished them.

Their bodies unused to the wicked winter
and 19 strong and fit healthy young men
fell and they fell and they fell and they fell and they fell
and they fell and they fell and they fell and they fell
and they fell and they fell and they fell and they fell
and they fell and they fell and they fell and they fell
and they fell and they fell again.

Here they lay in Seaford cemetery
with the smell of the sea and the prodding breeze
flesh, blood veins, long dissipated
I wonder where their spirits lie?
here in the land that took their young breath
or in their homeland

                in the swing and the sway and the sway and the swing
of the mango trees
in the thunder calls of the market ladies
selling their spices
in the hysterical laughter of little children
distantly related
in the lustrous sand squeezed in-between sinking toes
or in the frantic desperate howls
of their mothers and loved ones
when it was discovered they would not return.

Here they lay, Caribbean soldiers
from the British West Indies Regiment
thousands and thousands and thousands of miles
from home
fighting for a country
that was not theirs to fight for.

KAT: Next stop, main part of the museum, to an exhibition on West Indian, First and Second World War soldiers. One thing catches my eye; it's a picture … A picture of a group of black soldiers, sitting in front of their barracks at North Camp Seaford, Sussex, 1915. I look closely at the picture hoping to see some family resemblance; a curve of the forehead, the thickness of a bottom lip, or the tiny trademark François ears.

SCENE 10

"Never felt cold like this" 1915

LAZARUS [*Kat is marching.*]

    1, 2
    1, 2
    1, 2, 3, 4
    Never felt cold like this, never felt cold like this.
    Never felt cold like this, never felt cold like this.

    1, 2
    1, 2
    1, 2, 3, 4
    These boots are too tight, too tight, too tight.
    These boots are too tight, too tight, too tight.

    1, 2
    1, 2
    1, 2, 3, 4
    The locals are waving, smiling, waving.
    The locals are waving, smiling, waving.

    1, 2
    1, 2
    1, 2, 3, 4
    We yet to receive any pay.
    We yet to receive any pay.

    1, 2,
    1, 2,
    1, 2, 3, 4
    Doing this is for King and Country.
    Doing this is for King and Country.

    [*Kat stops marching.*]

I miss Dosue
her sweet smile, her warm embrace
wish I'd slipped a ring on she finger before I left
to show her how much I loved her.
I'm a jolly West Indian soldier
as jolly as jolly can be
but I cold, cold, cold
from my eyes, to my ears, to my nose
I cold, cold, cold
Right down to my frostbitten toes.

SCENE 11

"Morning, Morning, Morning" 2009

[*Slide of Grenadian countryside displayed.*]

KAT: I land in Grenada and head straight to the tiny village of River Sallee in the parish of St Patrick. The first thing I do is go for a run.

> Morning, morning, morning
> this is the land where
> my slave ancestors resided
> this is the land where my blood
> has lived and died for generations
> this is the land where Lazarus
> once walked and talked and breathed.
>
> Morning, morning, morning
> shit that cow is huge, better be careful
> it's just standing in the middle of the road
> just staring at me
> go round, go round, go round Kat
> everything moves slowly
> and I mean slowly
> no one rushes for anything
> I am the fastest thing around here
> and I can assure you in this heat
> I am not going very fast at all.
>
> Morning, morning, morning
> the locals look at me as if I am crazy
> but they soon get used to me
> and I get used to them
> news of the route I have run
> will travel back before I do
> this is as rural as it gets
> no large supermarkets

public phone boxes, cinemas or Internet cafes
Lord there's a dog, it's barking
keep calm, keep calm, phew it's chained up.

Morning, morning, morning
sleepy and quiet
Lazarus wouldn't find it much different
from the River Sallee he left behind
morning, morning, morning.

SCENE 12

Birth Certificate Search

KAT: First mission, obtain a birth certificate. I head to the capital St George's, to the department of deaths and births, wait a while to be seen, remind myself to be patient, that I am not at home, in a can't wait to get where I'm going quick enough, get out of my damn way, been waiting for a least five minutes London vibe. Need to slip into a Caribbean, easy going flow; it was hot even in an air-conditioned building, started sweating like a beast, luckily I have my trusted wet wipes with me, slow Kat slow, slow Kat slow.

Yes, finally it was my turn, but they can't help. Disappointment, they only keep records as far back as 1904. Hope restored, they send me to another department, come on Lazarus, cut me some slack, give me a little help na. Sweat continues to stream from my armpits, down my brow, legs stuck together, waiting, waiting, waiting; sweating, sweating, sweating. Position myself close to the fan so I do not melt into a large brown puddle.

Just in time someone approaches ... they can't help either; instant disappointment but they do send me off to Sauteurs, a town near to River Sallee, where there is a Catholic church and where Lazarus' birth may well have been registered.

[*Video footage is shown at this point of Kat in Sauteurs outside the Catholic church. In the video Kat describes meeting a woman, called Victoria (Vickers for short), who invites her into the church and shows her a number of old, large brown ledgers which go back to slavery days.*

These ledgers are records of births. Kat and Victoria search for Lazarus but unfortunately do not find any reference to him, but "Vickers" promises to keep looking.]

SCENE 13

The bus journey from hell and the National Museum

KAT: My next mission is to go to the Grenadian National Museum. I am hoping that this time, I will find something of use. I have been travelling around Grenada on these little mini vans, their equivalent to our buses ... imagine a tiny transit van, but no four wheel drive or power steering, everyone gets squeezed in and I mean everyone, even if there is no room but magically room is found, men, women, children, shopping, boxes of produce to sell at the market, no one is left behind!

Most of the buses are not in the best of condition, but they are cheap, get you where you need to go and make for a very lively local experience, so why not, but I never, ever, ever, take the mountain route across to town on the buses, for three reasons: one, the mountain route is very high and I'm scared of heights, two, the barriers to stop vehicles falling off the side are so damn flimsy they could not save a toy car, or are non-existent, and thirdly, some of the drivers drive thinking they are Formula One drivers and drive way too fast for my liking.

But the early morning bus from River Sallee back to St George's only took this route so I decide to brave it, ask Lazarus to keep me safe, after all I am doing this for him. The bus was already packed, I make my way to the back, take a seat and close my eyes hoping to sleep my way through the hour journey. As soon as the driver starts the engine, I knew I'd made a terrible mistake and that it would be a ride to remember.

Foot on full gas
he hurtles along the roads
flying over tarmac
as if he is the pilot of a small plane
I look at the locals, no one flinches
or bats an eyelid
obviously this was a normal experience for them
but I am an English born girl, used to traffic lights
zebra crossings, speed bumps and cameras
here there are none, it is a free for all
we swerve and sway up and down hills
and miss going off the sides of unrestrained precipices
by millimetres
he zips around corners, beeping loudly
to let on coming traffic know he is there
but does not think it was necessary to take his foot off
    the accelerator
panic rising
aware that at any given moment I might stand up
start screaming like a mad woman
and demand to be let out
but there is nowhere to go
we are at the highest point of the island
pray to God asking for deliverance
clutching the seat beside me
trying hard not to cry
because if anything goes wrong
I may only have enough time to say the Amen part of
    the Lord's Prayer
heart beating
throat dry
tears appearing
nail biting, inside praying, begging
that we will arrive safely
and not end up scattered into tiny pieces
at the bottom of a gully
finally after what seemed like an eternity
we reach

stomach heaving
hand shaking I quietly pay
both too traumatised and relieved
to put up an argument.

I fix my dishevelled clothes, make sure the nausea has passed and my hands have stopped shaking before I enter the museum.

Start to look around ... artefacts and information on the Arawaks, artefacts and information on the Caribs, there's Josephine Bonaparte's marble bath, antique rum making equipment, displays on the hurricanes and the under water volcano Kick 'Em Jenny. I run upstairs, modern art, some stuff on Maurice Bishop and the revolution in the eighties, must've missed the section on the First World War, it must be here, it must be here, it must be here somewhere.

"Excuse me do you have any more information on the First World War?" A female staff member looks at me and slowly shakes her head. I can't believe I'd just gone through a near death experience and there she is telling me she doesn't have any information. This wasn't a museum, museums have things in them, where was the stuff, the uniforms, the medals, pictures, letters, telegrams anything, anything at all?

She says, "Why you interested?" So I tell her, and the rest of the staff lean in and eavesdrops, fascinated.

She says, "You'd probably find more on the British West Indian Regiment in England than over here."

Lord I hope I didn't come across as rude or a snob.

She must've felt sorry for me as she goes into a draw and pulls out pictures of Grenadian soldiers before they left the Caribbean for England, marching, digging trenches, pictures of the crowds at the port waving off the soldiers.

She then pulls out a book titled, *The Grenadian Handbook 1945*. It contains a list of Grenadian soldiers who joined the British West Indies Regiment. Lazarus' name was there, we all got excited.

She says, "Leave me your details, and I'll get in touch if I find anything of use, and once you finish your research you must come back, you hear me, you must come back and let us know what you learnt."

This strikes me as funny that I would one day return to tell them about one of their own.

Call one of my cousins, to take me back to River Sallee, there is no way in hell, heaven or anywhere in-between that I'm jumping on another bus to go anywhere. Next time I visit I shall rent a car and take the low road everywhere.

SCENE 14

The Strike/Seaford Barracks October 1915

LAZARUS: Henry, Henry stop your foolishness, striking won't help, everyone's having the same problems, they said they would sort out the pay, give them a chance na, give them a chance. We all have family sitting at home waiting for money, everybody is in the same boat, you don't think I worried about my Dosue and my Theresa; of course I'm worried about them.

You're right, if the English boys getting paid, then so should we, if the English boys have decent barracks then so should we, if the English boys have good boots on their foot then so should we, but we should really try and reason with the English, talk to them, this kind of mad, mad behaviour will only get you in serious trouble.

Of course, I haven't forgotten about Nelson and the others, this is not what any of us expected, we all wanted to come and fight for the Motherland, but so far all we see is trouble, cold and strife, you're not the only one who's disappointed, it's not that I disagree with you, I believe in everything you saying, it's just that I can't agree with the way you going about things, this is a dangerous path you walking. These white officers don't joke, they not afraid to discipline at all, at all.

[*Addressing the audience.*]

October 19th, they take away Henry and about six Bajans. Henry just had a chance to grab some underclothes and that was it, they take him, put him on a boat and they ship him right back. How could they do that, I hear he end up in Trinidad and had to borrow a shirt from a friend when he reached, what kind of way is that to treat someone, the man was just expressing himself, telling them the truth about the harsh conditions we West Indians facing here. So what, we don't deserve the same treatment as the English man?

SCENE 15

Cousin Bertine 2009

[*Kat is running at the beginning of this scene.*]

KAT: The morning sun is racing me again, clocking up an eight miler, the terrain is tough, constant inclines pressure my calves, "Good morning, Good morning." I've toughened up a lot, no longer the whiney unsure runner, who left England almost a month ago, all this sunshine has done me good. I see Lazarus everywhere, in the breeze passing through leaves, the fresh scent sprayed by the ocean, in the mongoose, which cuts across my path, in the magnificent osprey I am lucky enough to see flying overhead.

Today mum is taking me to see cousin Bertine, hopefully I will find out something of use. Cousin Bertine is the closest I will get to Lazarus whilst in Grenada. When Lazarus failed to return, Dosue married someone else, and had more children, cousin Bertine is one of those children.

[*Kat stops running, slide of Cousin Bertine is displayed.*]

She lives in River Sallee, her house sits on a hill, high above a Baptist church. It is a Sunday, the church is packed, parishioners spill out onto the pavement, the hymns add the background music to our conversation, the view is stunning.

Grenada spreads out in front of me like a large bowl of tropical fruits, Cousin Bertine is over 90 years old, her mind is not as clear as it once was, she's hard to pin down, at times, slippery as a bluggoe skin and others as sharp as a cutlass but she welcomes us, happy to have visitors, happy to see my mother, whom she remembers as a child, in fact my mother used to send letters back to Cousin Bertine when she first arrived in England as a 14 year old.

She says Lazarus was a good man
She says Lazarus was a teacher
She says Lazarus always spoke his mind
She says Lazarus loved Dosue and Theresa
and that her mother never got over losing him
she talks, and talks and talks and is still self-conscious enough to be concerned about her appearance when my camera is whipped out.
She does not tell me much I do not know
but I sit quietly and greedily take in all she has to give
her voice soaks into my pores
I study every wrinkle etched deeply into her brown face
and watch her lips, intently
she reminds, me of why it is important to share stories and visit relatives before they become too old to remember.

SCENE 16

Egypt 1916

LAZARUS: Dosue darling, I hope you and Theresa are well, and that you've finally forgiven me for going away. Dosue I miss you girl, I miss you, I miss you, I miss you. We are in Egypt now in a place them call Alexandria. We leave England in a troop ship called the *Marathon* and it take us just over two weeks to reach, they say that ship come all the way from Australia, could you imagine, I would love to go to Australia one day, of course with you and Theresa by my side, I never leaving either of you again.

I wasn't sad to leave England, too cold out there, the winter biting you like a rabid dog. Supposedly it's much nicer in the summer. Shame I never get to see that.

Egypt now, Egypt is a different kind of place, all kind of scorpion, lice, spider, mice and snake to contend with. You're a very foolish man if you don't check your boots before you step in. Just the other day one of them young boys was screaming and bawling and shouting like a mad man, hopping from one foot to de other, one foot to de other, like a giant brown cricket ah, he did step on a lizard that was hiding in his boots, I tell you we did laugh and laugh and laugh and laugh, we does call him lizard boy now.

Egypt hot, the heat beating down on your head like a vex man, not like Grenadian sun, the sun here is oppressive, and so much sand, sand, sand and more damn sand, every time I open my mouth, I eating sand, it get in your hair, your eyes, your nose, your clothes.

Ever since we come the white officers have been putting us through our paces, marching, drill practice, musketry training, carrying, cooking, cleaning, building, digging, digging and more digging, manning the lines of communication and patrolling the Suez canal.

I don't mind the work but all of us boys itching, itching, itching for some action, to be in the middle of things, after all that's what we come for.

There's English and South African soldiers here as well, I've never seen so many white people in my life, I heard about dem, read about dem, even seen pictures, and before I saw a few with my own eyes, but look at me now surrounded by hundreds of them.

And if you think we struggling with the heat, you should see them, walking round red, red, red like giant crayfish.

Some of them white boys don't like us West Indians just because we black, silly ah, we fighting in the same war and they have problems with us, just because of our skin colour! Don't worry I'm keeping away from them, you know me always speak my mind, but I trying hard to stay out of trouble, especially after I see what they did to Henry.

Anyway I've made some good, good friends with Trinidadians, Jamaicans, Bajans, St Lucians, Guyanese, St Vincent boys and we get along real well. We set up cricket matches, play dominoes and cards, and even have boxing matches, nothing serious, just a little fun.

Dosue I tell you, I looking forward to marrying you when I get back, well someone have to make an honest woman out of you and since you have my child so it might as well be me, ok, ok, fix your face, I can see you pushing out you bottom lip all the way from over here, I just making joke with you.

Sorry the money took so long to reach, all kinds of problems was going on with the pay, I hope you and Theresa don't have to struggle too much, remember don't be too proud, go and ask my parents for anything you need, they will happily help you, you know how much they love you and Theresa.

Please kiss and hug Theresa for me, and tell her, her poppa loves her, make sure she don't forget me, Dosue just wait for me, just wait for me nah and I promise everything will be just fine.

SCENE 17

Lazarus Egypt 1916 / Kat 2009

[*Kat starts running.*]

KAT: 15 miles is the target for today; it will be the longest I've ever run and an intimidating distance. Yesterday I received a call from Vickers, the lady at the Catholic Church in Sauteurs. She'd not had any luck in locating a record of Lazarus' birth, she said she would keep looking, but I could tell by her voice she had already given up hope.

Five miles, starting to tire, the sun had played a cruel trick; risen way too fast, sweat my constant companion is streaming along my face and stinging my eyes, I carry on trying to place one foot in front of another, aware that if I let myself slip into despair this run will become a very painful and emotional experience.

Seven miles in, half way, not in good shape, starting to flag, energy being sapped with every languishing step. I've taken a coastal route; the views are impressive, green lush land, bright blue skies, shimmering blue seas, but might as well have been in inner city London as I do not have the will or the want to appreciate it.

[*Kat starts boxing.*]

LAZARUS: It was just meant to be a boxing match, a bit of fun, something for all the boys to have a bet on, and let off some steam, the English boy against me, but he called me a black bastard and the N-word, he said that a black man could never be an English man, even if he was born and bred on English land.

He said that I was stupid, no better than a monkey, he made monkey noises so everyone could hear and everyone could see, he questioned my loyalty, my intelligence and my bravery, said I was good only for savagery, that I could never be a soldier, I was only here, to cook, clean, carry and to dig, to scrub clean the white man's latrine, to shut up and never be seen.

[*Kat starts running.*]

KAT: Eight miles in, struggling, groin aching, heat beating down like a hammer, come on Kat, come on, come on Kat, come on.

Mile nine, I am no longer running in a straight line. This is a nightmare, I can, I will, I am, I can, I will, I am.

Mile ten, my feet are still moving, but I've lost focus, all I can think about is how little I've learnt about Lazarus.

[*Kat starts boxing.*]

LAZARUS: He said us West Indians have way too much pride, needed taking down a peg, stripped down to size. So I hit him and I hit him and I hit him and I hit him.

[*Kat starts running.*]

KAT: Mile eleven, this trip was a waste, a waste of time, a waste of money, a waste of energy, what the hell am I doing, running in this ridiculous heat?

Mile twelve, I just want to stop, I really, really want to stop, I just want to stop, I really, really want to stop.

[*Kat starts boxing.*]

LAZARUS: And I hit him and I hit him, until blood was running along his face,

[*Kat starts running.*]

KAT: Mile thirteen, just keep putting one foot in front of another, just keep putting one foot in front of another.

Mile fourteen, maybe it's me, what right do I have to tell his story? Maybe I'm not smart enough, intelligent enough, creative enough.

[*Kat starts boxing.*]

LAZARUS: I hit him and I hit him, until he stopped spewing, ugly hateful lies.

[*Kat starts running.*]

KAT: Mile fifteen, this is torture, whose stupid idea was it to run the marathon anyway, why would anyone do this to themselves, where the hell are you Lazarus?

[*Kat starts boxing, then falls to the floor, exhausted.*]

LAZARUS He called me a black bastard, and the N-word, so I hit him.
I'm a jolly West Indian soldier as jolly as jolly can be.
I'm a jolly West Indian soldier as jolly as jolly can be.

SCENE 18

Waiting, Waiting, Waiting 1916

DOSUE: Dear Laza,

I hope this letter finds you well, everybody missing you and everybody say hello, Theresa is so big now you would hardly recognise her.

[*To the audience.*] Bonjay no, no let me start again, Laza, how are you? Everybody miss you, I take Theresa to see your parents everyday.

Oh Lord why can't I do this, why can't I do this? Every time I try to write a letter, I just can't find the words, I have to start over and over again, and still I'm never satisfied with what I have to say, it sounds so, so stiff, but this one, this one I have to get right, it has to be special.

It will be almost a year since I've seen that man, and I just want to tell him how I really feel, I've been angry for too long, I want him to know that I still want us to marry as soon as he come back.

I want him to know
I regret not saying goodbye
regret not kissing him on his thick lips or
looking in his eyes
regret being so hasty and sending him on his way
regret being so full of vexness that fateful day.

Wish I could tell him
I miss the touch, the feel, the smell of him
the way his gentle hands would crawl around my waist
wish I could tell him
that I miss his fingers running through my hair

his tenderness, his kindness
but for some reason
I just don't dare.

You know what it's like when you love someone
you just can't seem to get them out of your mind
well my dreams are full of him
he is all I think about morning, noon and night.

I wish this pen would run freely
I wish this pen would run freely
I wish this pen would run freely
and tell him what I really feel
that I'm waiting, waiting, waiting
waiting for him to come home
that I'm waiting, waiting, waiting
with every ounce of my aching bones.

I wish I could tell him what I'm telling you
I wish I could tell him what I'm telling you
I wish I could tell him what I'm telling you
that I'm waiting, waiting, waiting for him to come home
that I'm waiting, waiting, waiting
for him to come home.

SCENE 19

Last day 2009

KAT: Today's my last day in Grenada and I am sitting underneath the large jade canopy of my favourite Tamarind tree, with a whole heap of little François cousins, reading them poetry and Anancy Stories. I tell my cousins all about Lazarus, the fact that he was our relative and that he once lived in River Sallee just like they do, and that he joined the Army and sailed to England, Egypt and to Kenya.

They excitedly ask questions like did he wear a uniform, what did he eat, what is England, Egypt, and Kenya like, what's it like to travel on a boat, did he have a gun? Then the words that Gran said came back to haunt me and I couldn't believe I had been too stupid to see it before. She was right, Lazarus did want me to raise him, to pass on his story to the next generation so he would never be forgotten again. My mind wanders back over all that has happened during this trip, I feel so much closer to Lazarus, as if he'd been with me every step of the way.

SCENE 20

Black Soldiers' Lament

[*Footage of BWIR soldiers marching in the Middle East, during WW1 is played at this point.*]

LAZARUS: In Egypt, stripped to the waist, and sweated chest
no reprieve for much needed rest
we dug and hauled and lifted high
from trenches deep towards the sky
non fighting troops and yet we died
by disease and illness
as we toiled, we marched, we worked
through sand storms and oppressive heat
through homesickness and heart felt pain
through memories of times gone
and through hope of what was to come
everyday bought new challenges
to mind, body and soul
as we tried to find our
way back to Islands which softly whispered our names
across vast seas
a black soldier's lament
is what I cry
of days spent
so far away
no clear blue water
to soothe tired feet
or friendly face to recognize
just pale skin
and harsh words spoken
just pale skin and strong wills broken

so as we leave Egypt behind
and as we sail towards Kenyan land
to a continent we once called home
the idea of being English slowly begins to disappear
as stories of African kings and African queens
fill our minds
and we start to question the Empire's Legacy
the brutality and the savagery
my head is not held as high as it once was
neither does my chest puff out
quite so prominently
my spirits do not soar
nor do my dreams fly as freely
no longer
naïve and carefree
but hope is restored
as lost sons return to claim lost shores
and I head for the true Motherland.
my mother's mother's, mother's mother's, mother's land.

[*This poem was inspired by, and incorporates some text from, the poem called "Black Soldier's Lament" by an unknown soldier of the British West Indies Regiment.*]

SCENE 21

Dosue: "Lazarus can't be dead" 1916

DOSUE: Bonjay, Bonjay, Bonjay, no you're lying, you're lying, you're lying, Lazarus can't be dead, he can't be dead, he can't be dead, I don't believe you, you're lying, you're lying, you're lying, what I go tell Theresa, what I go tell Theresa?

SCENE 22

So many stories to tell

[Slide of the Debt of honour is displayed.]

KAT: Lazarus is buried in Mombasa, Kenya in a Commonwealth War Grave. He died on the 8th August 1916, on the day he arrived; just shy of a year from when he first left Grenada. I was lucky enough to go to America, November 2011 and meet his granddaughter Joyce for the first time. I stayed with her for a few days and we both connected instantly.

She told me there was a plaque and other documents but they have been lost over time, she told me that her grandmother Dosue never got over his death, and that she would tell her stories as a child about the scraps Lazarus got in. She said her grandmother described him as a proud outspoken but kind man.

She told me that the only explanation that had ever been given for his death was that he was stabbed in the back as he slept on the boat, on the way to Kenya, supposedly after an argument with a white solider. I have found no documentation to prove or disprove this and I will continue to look, continue to search, continue to raise Lazarus.

[Slide of Lazarus' grave displayed.]

So many more stories to tell
so many voices unheard
so many memories hidden
fighting to see the light of day
time to blow oxygen back into deflated lungs
time to reinstate, re-invigorate
so many of our boys suffered and sacrificed

in the King's name
so many forgotten names, so many pains
so many footsteps yet to be uncovered
love, tragedies, and triumphs
old bones fighting to be reclaimed
families reunited
over time and distance
fallen soldiers of all nations deserve to be upheld.

Our Caribbean boys travelled far and wide
England, France, Egypt, Kenya, Mesopotamia, Palestine
they should not be forgotten
they should not be allowed to sink into oblivion
they should not be ignored
they should not be whitewashed from history
their courage and efforts denied.

So let's scatter historical seeds
which will plant and sow
and spread and grow
dispersing new wartime stories.

So many more stories to tell
so many voices unheard
so many memories hidden
fighting to see the light of day.

END OF PLAY

Additional poems by Kat François

When Mother Called They Came

When mother called her children came
When mother called her children came.

To the Somme, to the Somme, to the Somme they came
to the Somme, to the Somme they came
to the Somme, to the Somme, to the Somme they came
to the Somme, to the Somme they came.

From far, from wide
they came
from colonial lands
Sikhs, Muslims
Hindus and Christians
they came
many had never stepped foot
on English soil
but still they came
her children responded
to the call of their Mother
her trumpet bellowed
beckoning her scattered offspring
Canadians, Indians, West Indians, South Africans,
New Zealanders and Australians
feverish with pride and hope
filled with the excitement
and bravery of the young
as yet, untouched by the
reality of war.

When mother called her children came
when mother called her children came.

To the Somme, to the Somme, to the Somme they came
to the Somme, to the Somme they came
to the Somme, to the Somme, to the Somme they came
to the Somme, to the Somme they came.

They stepped away
from familiarity
boarded a troop ship
to an unknown destiny
they heard her cries and sought
to alleviate her maternal pain
racing across
foreign seas
to rescue Mother from tyranny
clink, clink
her children's tongues mix
clink, clink
her children's tongues mix
a spoon stirring a cup of English
yet Indian tea
the richness of Punjabi
the fast paced patter of West Indian patois
the distinct tones of the Southern Hemisphere
the singsong, twang of the Canadian accent
English but not British.

When mother called her children came
when mother called her children came.

To the Somme, to the Somme, to the Somme they came
to the Somme, to the Somme they came.
to the Somme, to the Somme, to the Somme they came
to the Somme, to the Somme they came.

The original version of this poem was commissioned for the BBC Radio 4 programme Front Row, and was written and performed on Friday 1st July, 2016 in Remembrance of the Commonwealth lives lost at the Somme.

One Hundred Years

100 years ago this very day
the chest of a British West Indian soldier
rose and fell for the final time
thousands of miles from home
away from the sound of his sea
from the familiar touch of his loved ones.
loud squawk of his seagulls
bubbling chitter chatter of his market women
naughty giggles of children he taught
sing-song ring of the school bell he rang.

Swapped for
tight boots
encasing tired feet
the British cold
shoddy barracks
booming gunfire
barked orders
marching, marching, marching
rolling waves
seasickness
homesickness
digging, digging, digging
merciless Egyptian heat
sand, sand and more sand.

Dosue's lips, he will not kiss again
nor will his toddler place her chubby hand
into his large palm.
River Sallee; his tiny village
will learn to live without him.

He is blanketed by foreign soil
warmed by a foreign sun

Grenada calls
she is a distant lover
waiting for his return
waiting for all her boys to return
but their bones have grown too old, too frail
dementia has set in and they have forgotten the way home

The Motherland called and he came
his mother called, cried and begged for him to return
but her calls fell on dead and buried ears.

Poem written by Kat François on the 100th anniversary of the death of Lazarus François 8th August 2016.

KAT FRANÇOIS

I am British born. Both my parents were born in the Caribbean on the island of Grenada, which is only 12 miles wide and 21 miles long.

Raising Lazarus is about my mother's side of the family.

My gran and mother grew up in a tiny village called River Sallee in the Parish of St Patrick. My family have lived in that very village as far as we know since slavery times.

My gran came to England in the 1950s seeking her fortune and a better life for herself and her children she was forced to leave behind in Grenada.

My mother joined my gran in England as a 14-year-old and like all migrants had to learn a new culture, a new way of talking and even a new way of walking.

Grenada is where the hero of my story was born and raised. It's been seven years since that revelation and with the help of my partner Robert Covell, we have searched for as much information as possible around Lazarus and Caribbean solders in WW1. The search goes on, as information has not been easy to come by.

At first, I was quite intimidated by Lazarus' story, I was not sure if I had the right to tell it or share his story and the thought of all the research needed was also intimidating. To be honest in the beginning, I did not know where to start.

The play *Raising Lazarus* has been a slow burner, as at first, I did not appreciate the importance and significance of his story and the story of others like him.

This soon changed when every time I performed the play, the encouraging reactions I received helped to steel my resolve. The positive reactions forced me to realise I had a right to tell his story and the stories of forgotten Caribbean soldiers. Not only did I have a right but as performer/poet/playwright and descendent of a WW1 solider, it was my duty.

Some of the most memorable performances I have had have been in front of family. I performed *Raising Lazarus* in Sydney, Australia in January 2016, a performance that was attended by my elder sister, who had yet to see the play. It was a special moment to bring my family history to such a far away place, yet have such a personal connection in the audience. A few tears were shed at the end. While there I discovered that Lazarus had travelled on the same ship, at a different time, as many indigenous Australian soldiers on their journey to the war.

A performance took place at Nottingham Playhouse in front of ten- to eleven-year-olds, who received the play very well and asked many questions during the Q and A session. They were also eager to share their own family histories with me. The performance also proved the scope for *Raising Lazarus* to be presented to a younger audience and I have subsequently created a 45-minute version with accompanying workshops and supportive teaching materials for schools.

I am now passionate about history and telling stories that shed light on those who have been forgotten. I am passionate about weaving history into palatable tales that audiences can relate to. This is the same person who daydreamed her way through history lessons in school ... if my history teacher could see me now! The irony is too glaring to ignore.

As an artist I look at it as my job to create art, which everyone can relate to, to present history in a palatable and respectful manner, which can hopefully elicit laughter, tears and ultimately inspire those who see *Raising Lazarus* to research their own family histories.

One of my greatest wishes would be to take the play *Raising Lazarus* back to River Sallee and perform the play in the very village Lazarus was born and raised and where much of my family still reside and of course to America to share a performance of the play with his granddaughter Miss Joyce and his great granddaughter Ava and other relatives.

The other wish would be to visit the gravesite of Lazarus François, which is in Mombasa, Kenya where he was laid to rest in a Commonwealth war grave site and pay my respects.

Thank you to all who support my work, thank you to all who support this important story. I move forward with the wish, hope and determination that this story can continue to travel far and wide.

For more information or to book the play, performances or workshops please go to katfrancois.com

www.ingramcontent.com/pod-product-compliance
Lightning Source LLC
Chambersburg PA
CBHW031243160426
43195CB00009BA/587